Who ARE These People?

The Drawings of
Irv Bramberg

Compiled by his loving wife Joyce
Captioned by his kin and friends

Copyright © 2008 by Joyce Bramberg
All rights reserved. No part of this book may be used or reproduced in any manner whatsoever without the written permission of the publisher.
For information contact
Georginas World Inc.
PO Box 3170
Los Angeles, CA 90067

Published by
Little Red Hen Books
Los Angeles, California

printed in USA
ISBN #978-0-6152-0321-8

Book design by Chele Welsh

I knew Irv for almost twenty years before I found out he could draw. I knew him to be a sculptor and a man of impeccable manners, keen business acumen, delightful humor and stalwart devotion to his wife, my best friend, Joyce. But I didn't know he could draw.

Then one day I saw these funny pictures on their coffee table.

"Who are these people?" I asked Irv.

"I have no idea," he said. "They just show up on the paper when I'm not looking."

As I looked at the images, names and descriptions began to pop into my head. I wanted to know what these characters "said" to others, so Joyce and I sent copies of the drawings to Irv's family and friends and asked them to send us any captions that occurred to them. This book is the result.

Irv had been courageously battling cancer for over a year when we started this project. The first copy of the book rolled off the press the very afternoon Joyce called to tell me Irv had left us. At least he got to see, and approve, the final proof.

Make up some captions of your own. It's fun. Or pass the book around at parties and see who comes up with the funniest, pithiest, or most profound thoughts that these "friends of Irv" might be having.

AND, as Irv would say, enjoy.

Chele Welsh
(One of Irv's friends.)

Frankie never met a get-rich-quick scheme he didn't like.
Spends a lot of time at the track.
Is very good to his mother.
                                        Chele Welsh

Had a date about six years ago.
                                      Rafael Mauro

Who #1

Who #2

Bernard would love to whistle at girls.
He plans to do just that — when he's older.
Rafael Mauro

Leonard has always wished to be taller.
He compensates by generous kisses to women's navels.
Bob Richter

Johnny just loves his Uncle George — who flashes the cash.
Marsha Meyers

If you can smile when all around you are crying,
you don't have a clue about what's going on.
Harriet Belkin

Do you REALLY think I'm beautiful?
Donald C. Mitchel

Who #2

Freddy's "bedroom eyes" have been frequently blackened by jealous husbands... and discerning wives.
Bob Richter

Herman practices the art of shyness to cover his mother's influence concerning his social life.
Rafael Mauro

Roger: Salesman of the month!
Marsha Meyers

Earl hopes the wedding planner won't find out he doesn't know the bride — or the groom.
Andrew Robinson

Who #3

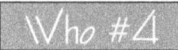

Erwin at age six was taken to H.M.S. Pinafore, and has never fully recovered.
              Ken Stone

I'm the Decider.
    Renny Temple

Trust me.
   Donald C. Mitchel

Bill — ever the blind date king.
        Marsha Meyers

Warren tried being gay in the military and failed at both.
                Raf Mauro

Frankie's never met a martini he didn't like.
             Andrew Robinson

Who #4

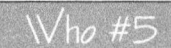

Mr. Melman, high school chemistry teacher:
                every kid gets a "C."
                          John Welsh

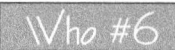

Of COURSE they'll vote for a woman!!!
Donald C. Mitchel

Frieda LOVES to lunch with The Girls.
Marsha Meyers

Lydia will search your medicine chest, scrutinize your wardrobe, and exaggerate any rumor that passes through her.
Bob Richter

Evelyn wishes she had a secret.
Raf Mauro

I found my keys — and then I forgot where I parked the car.
Harriet Belkin

Who #6

Do you really expect me to know?
Donald C. Mitchel

Henry - the science geek - finally finds the answer!
Marsha Meyers

Ralph, an accountant, always wanted to be an airline pilot.
His eyesight prevented his achieving his dream,
but he married rich.
Bob Richter

Simon was told the meaning of life,
but it somehow slipped his mind.
Raf Mauro

I'm going to get my psychology book... If I can find my locker.
Harriet Belkin

Who #7

Who #8

Alan has a nasty habit of looking thru peoples drawers.
Marsha Meyers

Al's crooked grin is charming to many of the ladies.
He frequently does an impression of Harrison Ford.
Bob Richter

Joel actually IS holier than thou.
Raf Mauro

Have I got a deal for you!
Harriet Belkin

Who #8

Ivan — born again.
              Marsha Meyers

Danny's enthusiasm is exceeded only by the degree to which others try to avoid him.
                                      Bob Richter

Who #10

Albert — sweet guy — except behind the wheel.
Marsha Meyers

Oscar dreams of world domination...
    Or at least a date for Saturday Night.
Ken Stone

Why do you think I'm the one who ate the last doughnut?
Caren Kaye

Filbert takes children's tricycles whenever possible.
Raf Mauro

Where's my dough? I'm gonna break your legs...
Harriet Belkin

Who #10

Who #11

Al decided to be Alice for a while.
          Caren & Renny Temple

Veronica is still hoping she'll break that glass ceiling.
               Marsha Meyers

Wrong! That's "whom."
    Harriet Belkin

Kevin's been playing the part for so long,
   that he's come to believe he really is Liza Minnelli.
                Meredith Robinson

Who #11

Tisha loves it when people tell her she looks like Merel Streep.
John Welsh

Iris can absorb pastry (Hungarian pastry) through her skin.
Raf Mauro

Who #13

When Mabs plays Bingo, she plays to win.
Ken Stone

The beauty of growing old is
    your husband has terrible eyesight too.
Caren Kaye

Clara: the critic. Nothing is ever right.
Marsha Meyers

Go away and play under somebody else's window.
Harriet Belkin

Who #13

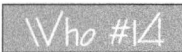

Is it hot in here or is it just me?
        Caren and Renny Temple

Glen gets a lot of satisfaction out of raising rabbits.
            Marsha Meyers

Jasper is taking a home-study course in how to be a clown.
              Raf Mauro

Tag! You're IT!
  Harriet Belkin

Who #14

Who #15

Ralph sells insurance -
    but only until his career as a rapper takes off.
                                                Ken Stone

Thomas, the aspiring politician, tried talking out of
    the side of his mouth for a while.
                                            Renny Temple

"No, Uncle Arthur was real. I should know,
    I played him on Bewitched." (Paul Lynd)
                                        Meredith Robinson

Phil knows a lot of people who are almost famous.
                                            Raf Mauro

It's totally rebuilt — a great car for you.
                                    Harriet Belkin

William F. Buckley? The man's a giant!
                        Now, pass the Scotch.
                                        Andrew Robinson

Who #15

Who #16

Nick believed the man he met at the pub who told him that if he stood very still pointing North for three days, while allowing a bird to perch on his wrist, a man in a black hat would give him a million dollars.
         Meredith Robinson

Oh LOOK! There's MADONNA!!!
         Donald C. Mitchel

Adolf kept trying to perfect his salute.
         Renny Temple

Stanley plans to become a symphony orchestra conductor as soon as he learns to read music.
         Chele Welsh

Everybody...stand up and sing the National Anthem, followed by the Pledge of Allegiance,
    followed by "God Bless America."
         Harriet Belkin

Hey, didn't we meet at Woodstock? Woodstock Two? No? Okay! Catch ya later!
         Andrew Robinson

Who #16

Chester plans to write his memoir while he does his time.
                                                    Chele Welsh

Butch is looking forward to having sex with
          someone conscious some day.
                                        Raf Mauro

Who #17

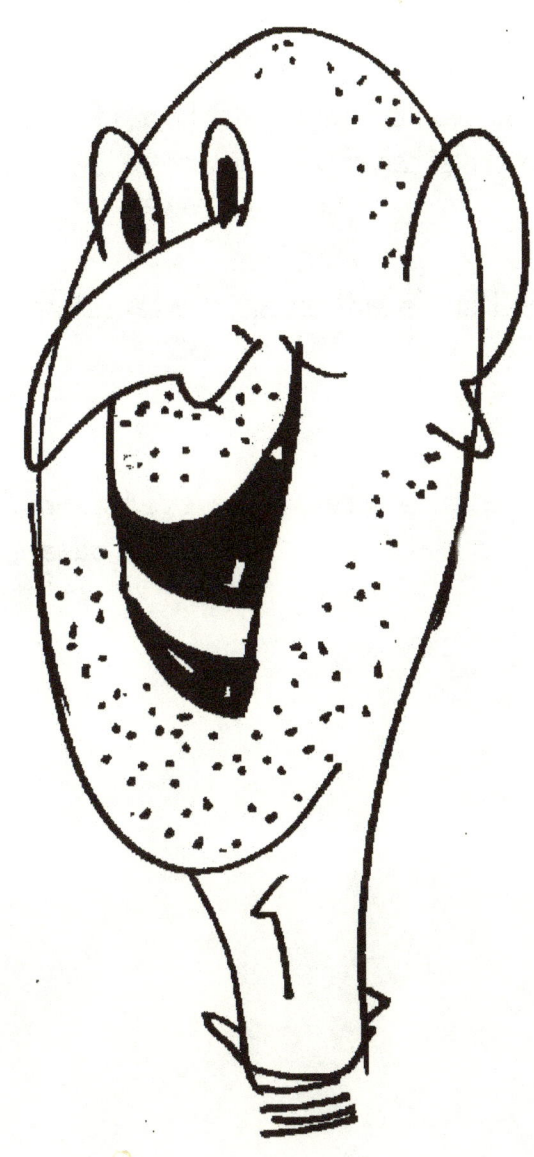

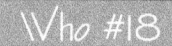

Bradley, alas, was convinced that human flight was only a matter of will power.
                          Ken Stone

Sometimes Harry's enthusiasm overtakes him.
                          Chele Welsh

Alfie practices running to greet a loved one deplaning - just in case.
                          Raf Mauro

Who #18

Who #19

Algernon is having an identity crises!
　　　　　　　　　　　　　Chele Welsh

"It's a look. I'm going for a look."
　　　　　　　　　　Raf Mauro

Who #19

On entering a room, Rhonda never fails to spot the hors d'oeuvres.
Ken Stone

Sweet Aunt Carmen, always has a toffee in her pocket for a child.
Marsha Meyers

Hi. My name is Hepsabah and I'm an alcoholic.
Harriet Belkin

Henrietta is delighted by the sight of frilly under garments.
Raf Mauro

Luella nabs the last shrimp cocktail at the Christmas party.
Andrew Robinson

Who #20

Leonard only knows one joke, as all his friends can attest.
                                                    Ken Stone

I went for a walk, and I can't find my house.
                                              Harriet Belkin

Ronald will never refuse a drink.
                              Bob Richter

Who #21

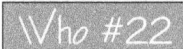

Agatha gets a bit aggressive when politics is discussed.
Chele Welsh

Mrs Chandler doesn't wear hats just to get attention.
Raf Mauro

Who #22

Ambrose likes a bit of aggressiveness in his women.
Chele Welsh

Bernie never hesitates to ask, "You gonna eat that?"
Raf Mauro

Who #23

Who #24

Roger prefers to be called "Spike."
　　　　　　　　　　　　　Chele Welsh

(And yes, he DID win the spitting contest.)
　　　　　　　　　　　　　　　Raf Mauro

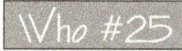

Lilly will be crushed if you don't compliment her on her new hair style — and so blasé if you do.
                                                Ken Stone

Marissa is fashion challenged — still believing in "high hair."
                                                      Marsha Meyers

Bernice has never met a man she didn't like.
                                        Bob Richter

Gossip? Who, me?
            Harriet Belkin

Who #25

Who #26

Fenley is sometimes just a little too darn easy going.
　　　　　　　　　　　　　　　　　　Chele Welsh

Archer knows that he knows more than you do —
　　except about women.
　　　　　　　　　　　　　Raf Maufo

Who #26

Agatha has always had a fine sense of style.
           Chele Welsh

Mildred is addicted to hot oil hair wraps.
           Raf Mauro

Madame Sitkatski maintains that Luella getting the last shrimp at the Christmas party doesn't bother her a bit!
           Andrew Robinson

Who #27

So we're both members of Mensa?
        (Perfect match thought Audrey.)
                                    Caren Kaye

Pam has a small problem with alcohol... It makes her giggle.
                                    Marsha Meyers

Amelia hopes to be an intellectual one day.
                                    Raf Mauro

Hilly finds it just adorable that her neighbors, the Borks, "splurged" on a C-class Mercedes.
                                    Andrew Robinson

Who #28

Frances never heard a rumor she could keep to herself.
Marsha Meyers

Frances is easy.
Bob Richter

Susan classifies men by their hair style.
Raf Mauro

Frances always enjoys subtle innuendo...
as long as it's not too subtle.
Andrew Robinson

Who #29

Charlene just can't hide her admiration
for the new UPS delivery boy.
Chele Welsh

Who #30

Who #31

Vincent can arrange just about anything.
                                    Chele Welsh

He went that-a-way.
            Donald C. Mitchel

Who #31

Don — the pastrami king!
                        Marsha Meyers

That sex drug makes me bulge in the wrong place!!
                                                          Caren Kaye

The Colonel, after his retirement from the service,
        continues to order those about him.
                People make obscene gestures behind his back.
                                                              Bob Richter

No, you can't join the club. You're too ugly.
                                        Harriet Belkin

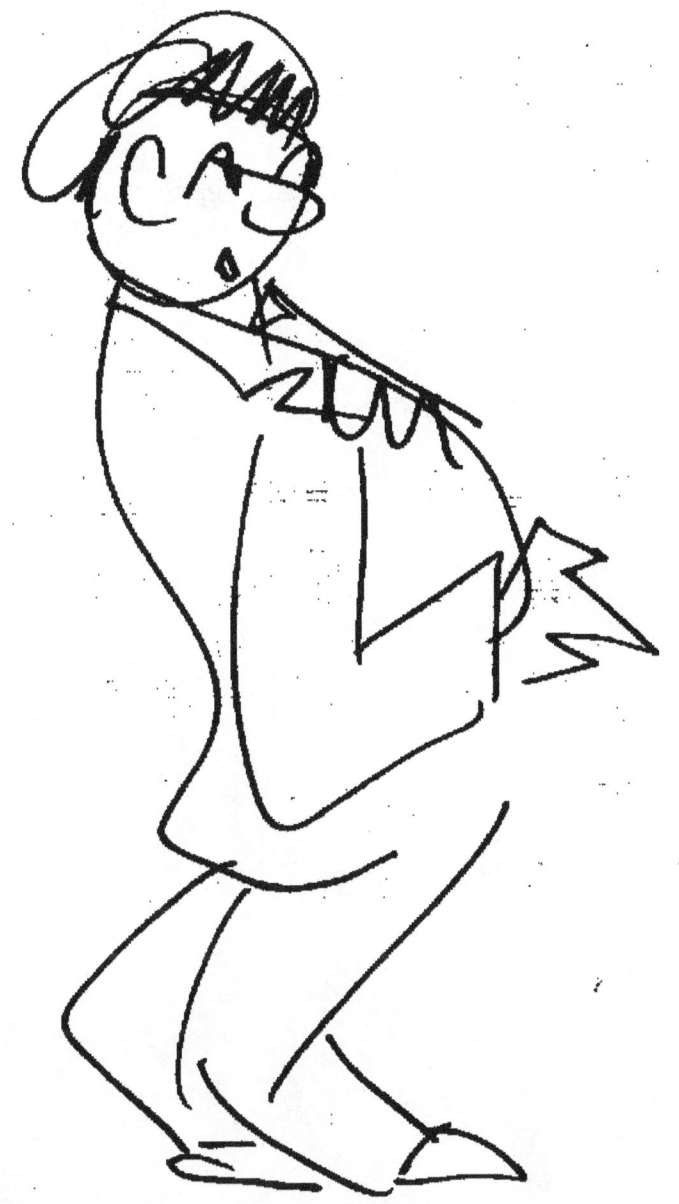

| Who #33 |

Mr. Bombasky does not suffer fools lightly.
          Chele Welsh

OK. Who farted?
    Renny Temple

Who #33

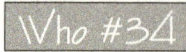

"The theory of relativity? Jah..
    That's when all your relatives haff annoying theories."
Andrew Robinson

Professor Glimp has misplaced his keys - - - again.
Chele Welsh

Who #34

Who #35

Terrence is the top closer in his sales group.
                                        Chele Welsh

How many Rabbi does it take to finish a story?
                                        Caren Kaye

Who #35

Who #36

Byron has put his left foot out...
    but he is still unsure of just what it's all about.
        Chele Welsh

Who #36

Hey, you guys...
Yeah you:

Andrew Robinson
Bob Richter
Caren Kaye
Chele & John Welsh
Donald C. Mitchel
Harriet Belkin
Ken Stone
Marsha Meyers
Meredith Robinson
Raf Mauro
&
Renny Temple

Thanks for clearing this up for me.

Irv Bramberg

www.ingramcontent.com/pod-product-compliance
Lightning Source LLC
Chambersburg PA
CBHW031418040426
42444CB00005B/625